# Preston, Bowleaze and Overcombe

# Preston, Bowleaze and Overcombe

*D. Joan Jones*

Roving Press

Published by Roving Press Ltd
4 Southover Cottages, Frampton, Dorset, DT2 9NQ, UK
Tel: +44 (0)1300 321531
www.rovingpress.co.uk

First published 2012 by Roving Press Ltd

ISBN: 978-1-906651-145

British Library Cataloguing in Publication Data
A catalogue record for this book is available from the British Library

Cover design by Tim Musk

Set in 11.5/13 pt by Beamreach Printing (www.beamreachuk.co.uk)
Printed and bound by Henry Ling, at the Dorset Press, Dorchester, DT1 1HD

To my beloved husband,
with grateful thanks for his help and patience.

# Contents

# Preface

To be able to study and research the history, growth and development of Preston across the centuries has been a fascinating and revealing experience. There has been so much knowledge and information to uncover and gather from this forward-looking, active and co-operative community. With the busy lives we lead today, the history of a place together with its development, surroundings and neighbourly relationships can be easily overlooked. My aim has been to uncover, through research and conversation, the wealth of interesting information and past events that make Preston what it is today.

During the writing of this book I discovered that some people in Bowleaze and Overcombe prefer to remain separate, while others were greatly interested in being included and wanted to learn about the wider area. In spite of a range of maps, including Ordnance Survey maps in the Dorset History Centre in Dorchester, and careful research undertaken at Weymouth Council Offices by a local councillor, there appears to be no official boundary defining Preston. Therefore it was decided to embrace both areas (Bowleaze and Overcombe), respect their individuality and hope that what had been researched and written would be accepted and enjoyed by all.

**_D. Joan Jones_**

# Acknowledgements

Grateful thanks are extended to so many interested and generous local folk who helped with the book, including the following:

Mrs J. Balem, Mrs A. Barnes, Mr & Mrs C. Baston, Mr J. Bolton, Mr M. Browne, Mrs W. Buckingham, Mrs H. Burridge, Mr & Mrs M. Clements, Mr P. Evans, Flora, Mrs A. Fox, Mr & Mrs G. Frazer, Miss H. Galling, Mr T. Garret, Mrs B. Gilmour, Mrs J. Harris, Mr & Mrs G. Jones, Miss B. Jones, Miss L. Jones, Mrs C. Joy, PC C. Joyner, Mrs V. Lucas, Mrs J. Madge, Cllr & Mrs Mannings, Mr L. Mansell, Mr Marsden, Mrs L. Martin, Mrs G. McAuley, the late Mrs R. Moss, Mr A. Penman, Mr R. Price, Mr R. Ross, Mrs V. Russell, Mr & Mrs Scriven, Mr J. Sweetapple, Rev. T. West, Mrs C. Willis, Mr N.G. Wilson, Mrs J. West.

I would also like to thank all those who supplied photographs including Mr & Mrs C. Baston, Mr B. Hayter, Mrs P. Henshaw, Mr J.R. Jones, Cllr & Mrs Manning, Mr I. Ross, Mr B. Serle, Mrs Peggy Simpson and Mrs Alex Sissons. Also those at the Dorset History Centre and Julie and Tim Musk at Roving Press, without whose help this book could not have been compiled or published.

Ordnance Survey area map (approx. 1970).

# Introduction

The book is divided into sections covering the areas of Preston, Overcombe, Bowleaze Coveway, Chalbury Corner, Seven Acres, Telford Recreation Park, Littlemoor Road, Coombe Valley, Wyke Oliver Road and Lodmoor. The text starts with St Andrew's Church and the origins of Preston. Then imagine setting out on a long-distance walk which has been divided into stretches, in between which a rest is taken with an opportunity to look around and consider other things. So, leaving Weymouth on the A353, one way leads along Preston Beach Road to Overcombe Corner. Here the road forks right, continuing uphill and along Bowleaze Coveway. The next requires a return to Overcombe Corner where the A353 continues along Preston Road to the roundabout at Chalbury Corner. From here we continue along Preston Road to Seven Acres Road, with a brief diversion to Telford Recreation Park. A further route runs up to Littlemoor. There is also a winding country road up Coombe Valley. This leaves Wyke Oliver Road to be explored, followed finally by a walk around Lodmoor Nature Reserve.

Attention has been focused on both adults and children, including those born in Preston and 'incomers'. It is hoped that the reader will find not only memories here, but also events and observations of fresh and unexpected interest.

Enjoy your walk!

# Chapter 1

# The Origins of Preston: An Ancient Church

The *Domesday Book* of 1086 has Preston spelt as Prestetune and referred to as a *vill* situated near the sea, west of Osmington. In 1228, Preston was recorded in Old English texts as *Preost-tun* meaning 'the farmstead of the priest', indicating that a dwelling, farmland and church were established there. Later, in 1285, Preston was spelt *Prestone* and finally as *Preston* in 1291. At that time Preston was not a village; it was the area where the Sutton Poyntz church was built.

*Preost-tun* was classed as a prebendal (tithe) farm. From it, a tithe, or tenth of its produce went to the priest as his stipend or official income. In the Middle Ages, it was normally a rector who was the independent incumbent, and from the tithes and altarage he received he not only paid his vicar but also was responsible for the maintenance of the church. (Altarage was money paid to the rector when a parishioner received communion and also on the occasion of a funeral.) At this time, a vicar was generally an assistant clergyman coming from the lower classes but able to read and write and understand a little Latin. Whilst caring for the church and leading some services, he was paid from the rector's stipend. This distinction between a rector and a vicar no longer exists.

## St Andrew's Church

Famed Dorset historian Rev. John Hutchins, in *The Church in Preston*, states that 'the church was very ancient and seems probably to have been of considerable note; for in Dean Chandler's Register 1405 it is said to be dedicated to St Andrew and to have ten pensionary chapels belonging to it'. Preston today still has a prebendal stall in the choir of Salisbury Cathedral.

Over the centuries, a community developed around St Andrew's Church. Although there appears to be no structural remains of the first church, proof of its early existence is realised by the inclusion of its name in the *Domesday Book*. The first church may have been a temporary wooden structure, whilst

3

later stone-built ones probably originally consisted of no more than a nave, chancel and sanctuary. Dating the current church is difficult. The font is partly Norman with a Purbeck stone stem added from the Perpendicular period (14th and 15th centuries), but there seems nothing else to confirm the current structure as being Norman.

Since the small bridge in Mill Lane is now considered by some to be of Norman not Roman origin, it may be feasible to assume the Normans settled here around the 11th century and built a church. The original building may have fallen into disrepair during the Middle Ages when the population was drastically reduced by the Black Death. This was thought to have entered the country in 1348/49 from a boat docked in Melcombe Regis. Additional damage possibly followed during the Roundhead rebellion when Oliver Cromwell challenged the Divine Right of Kings and established the Commonwealth. Such was the continued deterioration of the church over the ensuing years that by 1858 the Rector Talbot Hastings Bendall Baker took upon himself responsibility for three-quarters of the cost of its restoration.

*St Andrew's Church 1961.*

During the Medieval period, the porch was an accepted area for the discussion and undertaking of business as well as an introductory phase to a marriage or christening before entering the church itself for the actual service. To the right of the main door is a stoup, a simple hole in the wall which, in centuries past, was filled with consecrated water which intending

4

worshippers used to cross and sanctify themselves prior to entering 'God's house'. Another 'hole' can be seen on the east wall of the porch, the purpose of which can only be surmised; it may have held a small crucifix or a holy statue upon which an oath, agreement or promise could have been made and witnessed.

The lectern in the nave is shaped as an eagle, the outstretched wings supporting the liturgical reading matter. The eagle's feet rest on a sphere that represents the world, since 'the Word of God' is intended to reach out to all. In a wall close by the lectern is an oblique hole through which the altar can be observed. This is a squint or hagioscope, a term coined by Victorian ecclesiologists to describe an opening through which an attendant clergyman and the officiating priest could synchronise the celebration of Mass at the high altar. In this way, members of the congregation sitting behind pillars were able to see and follow the service. The word *hagioscope* is derived from two Greek words, the first *hagios* meaning 'holy things' and *skopes* meaning 'a range of vision'.

St Andrew's Church still has a flight of rood stairs, indicating that a rood loft once existed there. A rood was a type of medieval screen which separated the nave from the chancel and bore the figure of Christ together, in some instances, with Mary and St John. Many such rood screens were later destroyed during the Reformation (16th century). The Church also has several interesting and beautiful stained-glass windows, close to which a dedication and an interpretation have been thoughtfully placed.

Outside and just to the left if facing the porch is a pair of dripstone corbels, one at each end of a curved arch over the old window. Small and easily overlooked, these two carved images, possibly dating from around the 15th century, depict a young woman spinning sheep's wool into yarn whilst, to the right, a man in a close-fitting hood, jacket and trousers stands with a monkey on his shoulder and a dog at his feet. He is possibly a strolling entertainer using the bell in his hand to attract an audience, and his animals are part of his act. The young woman is a 'spinster', a term used then for young, unmarried females whose

task it was to spin yarn prior to the weaving process.

To the south of the church is the graveyard. Although the majority of gravestones found in old churchyards rarely date from before the 17th century, people have been interred there for centuries. At one stage woollen shrouds were compulsory by law, since the woollen industry in Britain was in decline and this law aided its restoration. It was the custom upon burial then to cast a sprig of rosemary and yew into the grave, the former for remembrance and the latter as an aid to immortality.

Wealthy and influential folk were interred within the church building, their presence commemorated by a plaque or flat stone. As times became more prosperous folk could afford to purchase a plot in the graveyard for the family, placing a large stone cover over the plot and embellishing it with decoration and inscription. A few 17th-century gravestones can be found in St Andrew's churchyard, some flat-topped with simple motifs sadly now almost indecipherable due to centuries of weathering and long-established lichens flourishing there.

The 18th century saw gravestones taller than those of the previous century and decorated with carved angels, cherubs, hour-glasses, skulls, and Death gathering his flock with a reaper's scythe. Slowly it became accepted that everyone had a right to a separate plot in the churchyard with their grave marked with a suitable headstone

*One 17th-century gravestone in the churchyard is still legible, bearing the simplest inscription, with an interesting capital 'A' and strange combination of the letters T, H and E forming the word 'THE'.*

or memorial. Today, with space at a premium and cremation accepted, burial plots are small and simple but still treated with respect and loving care. For those who gave their lives during World War I and II, a memorial stands close to the church porch. The name of John Sephton who died during the Falklands Campaign has been added to the list.

Entering the church grounds it is necessary to pass through the lych gate (spelt *lich* in earlier times, a word stemming from the Old English *lic* meaning 'corpse'). It was here the corpse awaited the arrival of the officiating priest for, according to the 1549 *Prayer Book*, the initial burial ceremony had to be conducted before the deceased was carried across the church boundary onto consecrated ground prior to the main burial service. A photograph taken in 1819 shows St Andrew's Church with no lych gate, whilst the current one, constructed in 1911, with its roofed gateway and wooden structure, is understood to have been made from wood saved from the burnt-out Court House in Sutton Poyntz and a cottage in Bincombe.

John Constable, the 18th-century painter, sketched his friend, the Rev. John Fisher, preaching to the congregation of St Andrew's Church from the old two-tiered pulpit, which was later replaced together with the pews and galleries. Whilst honeymooning at Osmington vicarage, Constable also sketched and painted his famous masterpiece of Weymouth Bay from Bowleaze Coveway. St Andrew's was the church featured in the novel *The Trumpet Major* by Thomas Hardy.

## Churchyard flowers and yew trees

St Andrew's Church has occupied its site from as far back as the early 12th century at least, and it is possible that the site may also have been a sanctified area before this with a preaching cross marking hallowed ground. This implies that the ground on which the church stands today may be the original unimproved grassland where wild flowers once grew in abundance and variety.

In 2002 when a record was made of the wild flowers in the churchyard, a small area had been set aside and left unmown to encourage their growth and preservation. Primroses, daisies, snowdrops and dandelions were recorded there, together with a single meadow vetchling that had survived amongst the long grass which supported its weak stem. Also among the summer grasses were clusters of hedge bedstraw, ox-eye daisies and meadow cranesbill. Plants such as lady's

smock and stinking iris could have been relics of a medieval herb garden used by herbalists in the past for medicinal purposes. Within some old kerbed gravestone enclosures, navelwort, white bryony and creeping cinquefoil had successfully established small but thriving colonies where they grew unthreatened by choking grass. Navelwort, in company with ivy-leaved toadflax and pellitory-of-the-wall, inhabited the old stone walls, and one speedwell which, in common with whitlow grass, was using a gravelled area to set its roots. Indeed, throughout the year the churchyard boasted five different members of the speedwell family. In 2011 one of the old graves had two lesser-known wild flowers thriving there – petty spurge and white stonecrop.

Perhaps today, the value of churchyards where a small area is left undisturbed can be appreciated as guardians of the nation's wild flowers and the wildlife they attract. They are living museums which surely we should be at pains to protect, develop and cherish for the benefit of future generations.

Yew trees, which are considered to be our only native evergreen tree, are invariably connected with churchyards, and there are numerous fine specimens in St Andrew's churchyard. They are known to attain a great age, some judged to have reached several thousand years, yet this is impossible to prove since old specimens rot in the centre, thus preventing scientific analysis of the annual rings that facilitate accurate calculation.

The tree was once considered sacred to Hecate, Greek goddess of the Underworld, associated with witchcraft, magic and ghosts. The tree therefore had connections with pagan rites and rituals, but with the advent and spread of Christianity it was absorbed into the new faith. A directive from Pope Gregory in AD 601 decreed that this pagan symbol and its site should not be destroyed but retained, blessed and sprinkled with holy water to make it a focal point of Christian worship.

# The Four Margarets

It is a recognised fact that our English churches, whether they are grand and imposing or small and rural, are treasure houses of art and history. One such treasure can be found behind the bell sallies (ropes) in St Andrew's Church; this is the west window, otherwise known as the Margaret Coddington Window. Three Margarets are represented in this fine stained-glass design: the Margaret to whom the window was dedicated at the turn of the 20th century, and two female saints of the same name.

Margaret Elizabeth Coddington died on 22 July 1905, a few years before Kempe, the designer of the window. Very little is known about her, but considering the size of the window and quality of the workmanship, its purchase would have been costly, so it can be assumed that Margaret was surely a much-loved and cherished member of the Coddington family.

The figure on the left in the window is that of St Margaret, the virgin martyr, who lived during the 3rd or 4th century AD. She is depicted with both crown and halo and dressed in a richly decorated medieval gown and cloak. In her left hand she carries a long and simple cross, whilst in her right she bears a palm leaf, the symbol of a martyr. A large ring around the third and fourth fingers of her right hand is attached to a long chain that curves downwards to a captured dragon lying in submissive pose and staring into her face. According to legend, her father was a pagan priest in Antioch (southern Turkey) and on her conversion to Christianity he drove her from her home,

whereupon she became a shepherdess. Olybrius, the governor of Antioch, captivated by her beauty, sought to marry her but, when rejected, he denounced her as a Christian and she was subsequently subjected to a cruel catalogue of punishment and torture. At one stage she was reported to have been swallowed alive by a dragon, but the cross she carried damaged its throat and she was spewed out whole and unharmed. Her determination, courage and submissive behaviour were said to have had a great and positive influence on Christian converts.

This account varies considerably but her venture with the dragon is depicted in many churches both in Britain and on the Continent, the dragon supposedly the Devil in disguise. She not only was the patron saint of nurses, peasants and women in childbirth but also interceded for those on their death bed who called upon her to save them from the Devil. Since there is no reference to her in ancient liturgies she is thought now to be a fictional character. Her Feast Day on 20 July was eventually suppressed in 1969.

The second figure on the right in the window is that of St Margaret, Queen of Scotland. Wearing a crown and a richly bejewelled mantle lined with ermine, she is clearly of royal lineage and bearing. With the invasion and conquest of England by the Danes, the Anglo-Saxon royal family fled to Hungary where they lived in exile in the court of St Stephen. Margaret was born there in 1057, the daughter of Prince Edward and Agatha, a German princess. In these civilised surroundings, the young Margaret was reared and educated and the family eventually returned to England to the court of Edward the Confessor.

Later, in danger once again, this time from the Norman invasion in 1066, the family fled north to Scotland and the court of Malcolm III. At Dunfermline Castle in 1070, the pious and beautiful Margaret was married to Malcolm, whereupon she brought to bear a civilising influence not only upon her husband but also on the Scottish court. The marriage was a happy and fruitful one and she became noted for her service to the Church of Scotland and the founding of many churches and monasteries. Margaret of Scotland, usually represented carrying a small crucifix, was canonised in 1250 and made a patron saint of Scotland in 1673. Her feast day is celebrated on 16 November, the day on which she died in 1093.

In the left-hand corner of the window, a small but significant single sheaf of corn can be found. This tiny symbol indicates the value and importance of this window for it was made in the workshop of C.E. Kempe (1837–1907). Kempe was a respected Victorian master glass-maker, and many of his windows can still be found today in churches and homes throughout this country and abroad. His work, like that of his contemporaries Edward Burne-Jones and William Morris, was and still is highly valued. Kempe used as his logo a small single wheatsheaf, and whilst this was generally etched in the bottom left-hand corner, it sometimes has to be searched for.

Kempe died in 1907, and as he never married and had no heirs his firm was taken over by W.E. Tower and J.W. Lisle. With the change of management came a change in name to Tower and Co. plus a subsequent adjustment to the logo. A small black tower was added to the rounded top section of the wheatsheaf, presumably relating to W.E. Tower who became managing director. It is this latter logo that can be seen in the Margaret Coddington Window, thus marking it as a special and beautiful treasure of St Andrew's Church.

A fourth Margaret has left her mark on Preston. Today, there are many who enjoy a walk up onto the ridge above Preston and will know of a sturdy and well-used stone seat thoughtfully placed there from which one can rest and admire the view across the fields to Portland and the sea. This idea of a seat as a memorial to Margaret Hobson was proposed by her family, when, after a long battle against cancer, she died at the age of 55. The family was advised against a wooden seat and accepted instead the suggestion of a stone one for its durability.

*'Margaret', simply but expertly carved into the backrest, commemorates Margaret Hobson, and the seat is locally referred to as 'Margaret's Seat'.*

## *The Church Rooms*

It had been hoped that when the Victorian church school became empty after the new school was built, the land on which it stood could be purchased and the old school demolished in order to erect a much-needed church hall. Sadly the price was too high. However, after three long years of waiting, planning and saving, an alternative site was found in Church Road. The Church Rooms were finally opened in October 2001 by the Rt Rev. David Stancliffe, Bishop of Salisbury. It was planned as a non-institutional building which could cater for meetings, lectures, parties and other customary local events and is well used by the community. Much thought was given to its design and décor, with a large, attractive entrance hall, a well-equipped office, a dining area and large kitchen. The lounge was named after David Lovatt who worked

with the Rector to commission an architect but who sadly died before the church was opened. The main hall was named after Stan Bailey who gave a legacy to help the purchase of the land, and the small, quiet Jefferis Room after Kips Jefferis whose family also contributed to the project.

*The building is referred to as the Church Rooms not the church hall.*

## Bell ringing

Three of the oldest bells in the church were cast in 1629 and a fourth in 1671. Two more were added in 1952 on the coronation of Queen Elizabeth II, thus making a ring of six. Later, one bell not ringing true, it was replaced and, together with two new bells, a ring of eight was achieved in time to celebrate the Queen's Golden Anniversary in 2006. The heaviest bell weighs 13 cwt and its inscription reads 'At thy departure I shall sound and ring to bring thee to the ground'.

The bell ringers, keen and dedicated to the art of ringing, consist of male and female ringers and cover a wide age range. Each bell requires just one ringer, and although lighter than even the lightest bell, a ringer learns, through practice and guidance, how to overcome and manage the physical skill and strict concentration required to ring a bell properly and in sequence with other ringers. The bells are numbered 1, 2, 3, etc. according to the number of bells in the peal, the treble being at the highest pitch, the tenor at the lowest. Initially the bells are rung in consecutive order. This is termed a 'round' which can later be turned into 'change ringing' when the bells are rung according to the leader's instruction in a series of differing numerical orders — and concentration is paramount!

*All eight bells are tuned to sound the true octave (scale of F#). The three oldest bells have designs of roses, thistles, vines and crowns, and two are inscribed with the words 'God calls'.*

*This 1924 Derby-made clock mechanism in the bell tower of St Andrew's has three weights: one for the mechanism itself, one for the quarter chime and one for the hour chime. It used to be hand wound, the weights slowly falling to the floor of the church over the course of a week and having to be hand wound back up. The clock has been converted to electric winding and now the driving weights fall only about 6 ft before the electric motors are triggered to wind them up again.*

*St Andrew's ringers have both a leader and an instructor, and this lively group practises on Monday evenings. One of the joys these church bells offer to interested folk is not only the merry peal of wedding bells and the call to church but also a chance to follow change ringing and its varied sequences.*

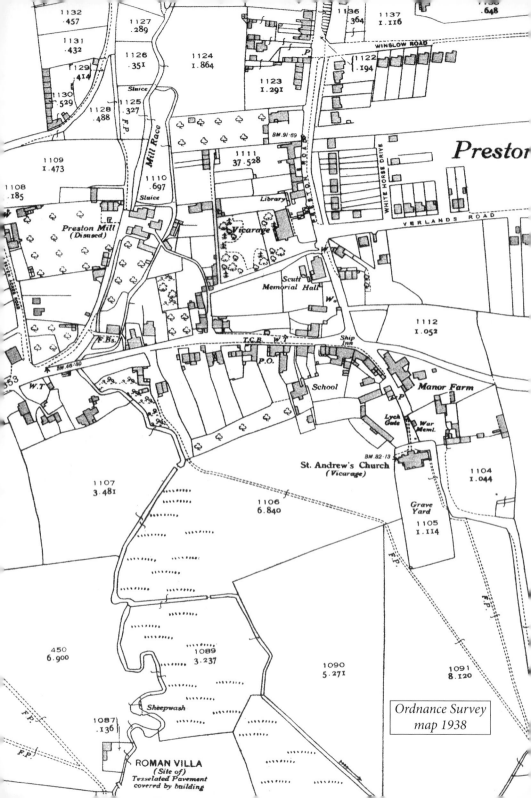

Ordnance Survey
map 1938

# Chapter 2
# Preston Street

"Preston has been nearly overwhelmed by modern development and caravans but there is a little of the old village left in the centre, including a few stone cottages."

(from *Dorset: The Complete Guide* by Jo Draper)

Reference to an early OS map dated 1902 indicates that the road from the church to Sutton Poyntz was once recorded as Preston Road which, at that time, was relevant since the church was then part of Sutton Poyntz and the road led only to the church. As the centuries passed and the population increased, more housing was required and small cottages were erected along a track that led down to the River Jordan. This became known as Preston Street, and what had previously been Preston Road was eventually changed to Sutton Road.

Before the 1920s houses for the village people were sturdy but basic, the stone walls thick and the roofs thatched. There were no bathrooms, just a bowl and a large jug of water in the bedrooms for washing, and a tin bath set out in front of the range downstairs once a week on bath night. Cooking was done in ovens either side of the range, a kettle full of hot water hung permanently close to the fire, and clothes were placed to air on a long overhead hanger. Laundry was washed in a large 'dolly' tub, mangled outside and spread out to dry on bushes and clothes lines. Irons were heated in front of the range, the handle of the iron covered to prevent burnt hands, and the base wiped clean before the act of ironing took place. There was no electricity or gas, and water had to be fetched from outside taps or the river. Toilets were situated in a shed at the end of the garden. Inside there was a wooden seat with a hole over a bucket that was emptied periodically on the garden as manure.

Sunday was a quiet day, when the children were not allowed to play outside but went to Sunday School where they learned to read and recite the Creed and the Catechism, after which the family, dressed in their best clothes, went for a local walk together. Later, when public transport became available, Sunday trips were taken to Swanage and Studland, and on Good

*Preston Village 1935*

Friday and Ascension Day the children went from school to church and then home for the remainder of the day.

With no motor transport in the village until World War I, the unmetalled road was adequate for the needs of the villagers. Pavements were not necessary and apart from bicycles, wagons and the horse and cart there was little traffic. Before 1826 a 'water splash' had been sufficient to ford the River Jordan, but with the advent of cars, motorbikes, trucks and lorries, it became necessary not only to widen the road but also to construct a bridge both wide and strong enough to support increasing and heavier traffic. With this widening of the road came the sad demolition of many dwellings across the road from the old Co-op.

*Preston Village 1951*

Small houses and shops lined both sides of Preston Street, with the original St Andrew's School positioned back from the road and behind the houses. Close by was Manor Cottage, a residence offered in former times rent-free by a gentleman in Preston to the grandfather of John Wesley, the Methodist. The house is still thatched, with straw pheasants perched today on top.

Toby Alfred and Ted Norris were both servicemen wounded in the 1914–18 World War, and when war ended they were set up in business as compensation and gratitude for their service. Toby Alfred ran his own cobbler's shop where he sold boots and shoes and offered repairs. Ted Norris lost a leg during the fighting, but because of his cheerful personality in spite of his horrendous war wound he was affectionately nick-named 'Happy'. He, too, became a shop-keeper and sold sweets, cigarettes, tobacco and bottles of 'pop' with glass marble stoppers.

Lamp glasses, wicks and paraffin were sold in the village until the 1930s when electricity was eventually installed. The green-grocer's 'shop' resembled a barn with vegetables and fruit laid out on long benches, and Miss Guppy, in her shop at the top of Preston Street, sold milk, butter and cream. Shopping was a daily chore since there were no refrigerators, only larders and stone slabs.

Once a week, the coalman delivered sacks of coal, the villagers supplementing it with wood and sticks for heating and cooking. Newspapers, including the *Dorset Echo*, were delivered daily by paper-boys on bicycles, the baker delivered bread and cakes by horse and cart every Friday, with the Co-op roundsman and the butcher taking and delivering customers' orders once a week.

Around World War I the Co-op was a small shop, but with a later purchase of adjacent houses it was extended and still serves the community today. It is still a well-maintained and busy local super-market. It is also part of the Co-operative Membership Community Fund which helps local groups as well as self-help organisations and charities. Every year in June and November, Co-op customers receive a share in the profits and these may be taken as vouchers which can be used in Co-op stores or paid directly into a bank; alternately, these shares can be donated to the Community Fund in Preston and money accrued is donated to local benefits. The Co-op has obeyed current Parliamentary demands regarding ease of access and shopping for the disabled, the main doors open automatically, and for customers with hearing difficulties a loop circuit has been installed, enabling them to adjust their hearing aids as they settle their bill at the check-out.

Established in 1991 and close to the Co-op, the Italian *Michelangelo* restaurant now stands where a grocery store stood before. A wide variety of pizzas and pastas are available in the restaurant, and orders from home are delivered free.

The first Post Office in the village is understood to have been set up in one of the thatched houses close to the Ship Inn. On the side of the house that faces the road, it is possible to trace a blocked doorway and a window, but the main entrance today stands at the side of the house. The stone walls are thick and sturdy, and the roof thatched and finished at the top with a skilfully executed, raised and elaborate ridge. In a corner of the wall that faces the road, about a metre above the pavement, a stone block can be seen. On this stone, two dates can be found – 1756 and 1778. Suggestions are that these may refer to the erection of the house and a marriage date, a feature apparently quite common at this time.

*Preston Post Office in the mid-1960s*

Sometime later the Post Office was transferred to the small general stores across the road and *c* 1998/99, when the shop was demolished, it moved yet again, this time to the SPAR shop. In its place, with separate garages at the rear, four small cottages were erected, sensitively in keeping with local style; they have been numbered appropriately 223A, 223B, 223C and 223D. Close by a dwelling bears the delightful name of 'On a Hill Cottage'. The attractive Old Vicarage at No. 219 is where Drs Pridham and Sloan once held surgery in their front room.

# The Rectory to the River Jordan

The original Rectory in Sutton Road was built in fine limestone around 1835. It was Georgian in design with the wording 'The Rectory' clearly written on the wall beside its entrance. In its long sloping garden, the annual church fete was held. Later a smaller rectory was built in the grounds of the old one, the latter adapted initially as a nursery and later as a pre-school group.

Almost opposite the old Rectory, Varlands Road leads eastwards and uphill. This was an old field name thought to have derived from the word 'furlong', which described the distance that could be ploughed by a team of oxen or horses before they required a rest; 220 yards equalled one-eighth of a mile and this was the furrow-long or furlong. The word *furlang* is Old English, with *furh* meaning a furrow and *lang* meaning long.

Scutt Hall is situated at the top of Sutton Road close to the old Rectory. It bears a plaque which reads: 'This hall was erected by Elizabeth Scutt in loving memory of her husband Charles Scutt, J.P. of Wyke Oliver AD 1909'. On the right-hand main gate a second dedication reads: 'These gates in memory of Elizabeth Scutt of Wyke Oliver who died April 18th 1929 were given by her daughter Mrs Florence Jenkins of 19 Overcombe'. Mrs Scutt's son also contributed financially to the church clock. Over the years the hall has been used for a variety of activities including Brownies, Guides, Scouts and Cubs, dances and dancing lessons, Mothers' Union meetings, wedding receptions, billiards, whist drives, socials, and rummage and garden sales.

Between the Rectory and the river several dwellings still sit snugly tucked away, and through this cluster of homes a footpath winds its way down towards the river. A sign on the Rectory wall indicates the direction of the weir below. Whereas today most folk read the word conventionally as 'weir' (pronounced as in *here*) some, whose families have lived in the area for decades, pronounce the word as *were*. This difference in pronunciation is interesting since 'were' stems from the Old English *wer* or even from Old Saxon *werr*, both referring to a dam across a river that regulates the flow of water upstream.

The old corn mill that stood close to the Mill House fell into disuse before World War I and was later used as stabling. The Bridge Inn, once thatched and known formerly as The Swan, has been enlarged and updated, with a car park for customers and a play area for children. High on the wall above the main entrance an unusual brick design represents the nearby bridge after which the inn was renamed.

The River Jordan is served by several streams flowing from the ridge

*Beside the narrow bridge that straddles the river is the original Mill House which is still inhabited and cared for.*

*In spite of its extensions and modernisation, the Bridge Inn retains the cosiness of an old local pub.*

above Preston. Some of the water in 1858 was directed from the pumping station to supply Weymouth. The river itself runs on under the road bridge to wend its twisted route towards the sea. After heavy rainfall the river rises and floods the area below the little wooden bridge and round the inn, but the riverbed has recently been dredged and deepened in an effort to alleviate this.

Between 1452 and 1531 the river's name underwent several changes, from Churdoneslade to Churdon, Jurdayne, Jordayne and now to Jordan. *Cerr* or *Cierr* (the *Ci* once pronounced as *ch*) was Saxon for 'a turn' or 'bend', whilst *dun* meant 'a hill'. A possible interpretation could refer to the fact that the river, running west from Osmington and finding it impossible to flow on and uphill, turned south towards the sea. Is this perhaps a more

*Roman Bridge 1907*

*Close-up of Roman Bridge today. This small stone bridge, now hidden by trees and shrubs, has for many years been thought of as Roman in origin, but recent controversy argues that it is of Norman origin. In-depth research by Claire Pinder, Senior Archaeologist in the Historic Environment Record in Dorchester, indicates that it is 'of uncertain provenance'.*

feasible interpretation of the word *Jordan* as opposed to its tenuous although understandable association with the Holy Land?

The old bridge over the stream was the start of a public footpath enabling pedestrians to avoid the narrow main road which had no pavements. At one stage, an iron walkway was attached to the side of the bridge and now hangs along part of the Buxton Road where it crosses over the old Weymouth to Portland railway

## *Some statistics*

Modern Preston was non-existent at the end of World War I and was for many years only a ribbon development along the Preston Road. The following figures from the Preston Population Census Count (Dorset History Centre) show how Preston has grown over the years.

| | | |
|---|---|---|
| 1801...385 | 1871...747 | 1941... data not found |
| 1811...447 | 1881...689 | 1951... data not found |
| 1821...508 | 1891...678 | 1961... data not found |
| 1831...555 | 1901...664 | 1971...3740 |
| 1841...672 | 1911...690 | 1981...4740 |
| 1851...711 | 1921...886 | 1991...4930 |
| 1861...723 | 1931... data not found | 2001...4860 |

*An influx of temporary visitors arrives in Preston. Kitchener's Army training camp, 1906 (from a postcard by AG Price, Week & Gimblett). .*

# Chapter 3
# Toll Gate to Overcombe Corner

Today, the word Preston on a road sign along Preston Beach Road (the A353) clearly delineates the boundary line between itself and Weymouth. This road was once, around the 18th century, a turnpike road with a toll gate house near Lodmoor at which a toll or fee had to be paid by all who used it. A toll was a tax or duty paid by users of the road towards its maintenance, and constituted a major improvement in the condition of the country's roads since Roman times.

Long after the toll system was dispensed with, the toll house remained, the last occupants being the Shorey family who also ran a horse-drawn cab service. An old milestone along the way indicated the distance to Weymouth as 1 mile and to Wareham as 17 miles. In 1965 the café at Overcombe Corner, on the left-hand side of the road going towards Preston, was demolished and replaced with a block of flats that overlook the bay and Lodmoor. About the same time the petrol station opposite was replaced with a hexagonal toilet block, and the road divided, turning left for Chalbury Corner and right for Bowleaze Coveway which was once the old route to Osmington.

*The Shell garage at Overcombe Corner was well placed for visitors to the area. Besides serving petrol, it offered Calor Gas, battery charging, cleaning and puncture repairs. The old coastguard cottages can be clearly seen in the background.*

*The café at Overcombe Corner in 1929*

A sea wall ran from the start of Preston Beach Road opposite Lodmoor to Overcombe Corner, *combe* being a short valley running up from the coast. This wall was built to separate the shingle beach from the road but

*Whereas some daring folk once walked dangerously along the narrow old sea wall, a wide and safe esplanade between the new wall and the sea now joins Weymouth promenade, the EC having contributed to the financial aspect of this substantial barrier.*

was frequently breached in winter's strong and sometimes violent moods, especially at high tide. This caused intense problems including diversions via Littlemoor into Weymouth and vice versa, plus the cost of repairs and removal of debris and damaged vehicles.

Eventually the old wall was replaced by the present sturdier one that slopes down to the road with a metal fence at its foot. Almost a mile long and reinforced with a steep bank of pebbles on the seaward side, this new stretch of road was given a 50 mph speed limit with one permitted crossing for pedestrians along the way. The esplanade is now a picturesque and interesting walk for old and young alike, especially parents with pushchairs and children on roller blades and scooters. It is not easy to differentiate between an esplanade and a promenade except that a promenade is defined as a paved, public walk usually beside the sea. The word is derived from the French *se promener* which translates as 'to walk' whereas an esplanade is a level piece of ground especially used by the public and is derived from the Latin *esplanare* meaning 'to make level'.

Originally, wooden seats were arranged along the esplanade with memorial plaques to lost loved-ones placed above. Due to wear and weathering, several

*Although the new seats have no back rest, the slabs, which have been cut from Portland Roach limestone, provide seating that will stimulate interest in the wide variety of small fossils found along the Jurassic Coast, including one group of specimens known as Portland Screws.*

of these much appreciated seats have been replaced with those of more durable limestone.

Occasionally in late spring you may see a female duck and her ducklings scurrying anxiously towards Lodmoor either along the esplanade or at the seawater's edge. It is possible for them to reach the safety of the nature reserve via a small tidal inlet which links with the reserve, thus avoiding the busy A353.

Turning left soon after entering Preston Beach Road from Weymouth, a narrow road leads down to the Household Waste Recycling Centre or 'the Tip' as it is generally called. Very few waste disposal sites like this one can boast an attractive approach road along which something is in bloom or berry throughout the year. Each spring there is white May blossom on one side of the road and vivid yellow gorse opposite. Also in one spring, an unusual though not rare plant was seen thriving along the wayside banks. This was dittander, a plant with white flowers and said to be found amoung the long grasses near the coast especially in the south. It made a pleasing and interesting show that year but hasn't been seen since.

# Chapter 4
# Bowleaze Coveway

At Overcombe Corner the road diverges, the A353 veering left to Wareham and right uphill to Bowleaze Coveway. On the right at the start of the hill is the Café Oasis, a busy place even through the winter. Nearby 'The Second Wind' caters for a variety of water-sportsmen including windsurfers, canoeists, kayakers and kite-surfers.

It was in this bay in December 1914 that two ships were caught in a storm so vicious and intense that even lifeboats were unable to make contact; fortunately no one was lost or drowned. Another threatened disaster in January 2008 caused the near grounding of the tanker *Marielle*, where, again, no lives were lost nor oil pollution caused.

In the mid-19th century a Coastguard station was established here to house the so-called Preventive Men, whose work entailed vigilance regarding smugglers, plus contact with passing or anchored shipping. The largest house was by the sea, occupied by the chief coastguard, and between his house and the cliff-face there was a signals room and an armoury. Built on unstable Oxford Clay, the coastguard cottages near the sea gradually succumbed to coastal erosion and were left derelict for years. Only two remain, modernised but still retaining their distinctive

chimney stacks. The remaining area has been sturdily reinforced with strong banking on which new dwellings have been erected.

In close proximity is the Spyglass Inn, previously called the Embassy. Refurbished and extended in open plan, it boasts a well-supplied carvery and areas where adults and children can dine together. In previous years children were not permitted in the bar but had their own indoor area with a pool table and dartboard, and refreshments were passed to them through a hatch. Today's children enjoy an outdoor play area whilst their parents can

*It was from the Spyglass Inn many years ago that the annual Boxing Day Pram Race was organised. A set of prams was kept throughout the year at the inn itself and on Boxing Day competitors, many in fancy dress, set off up the steep hill to the top and on down into Bowleaze Coveway where all had to drink a pint of ale, change places with their team-mates and run back. The remainder of the day was spent in seasonal celebration.*

dine and drink indoors or out. On one wall inside is a fascinating piece of modern art created from a cluster of coloured, large and cleverly flattened glass bottles.

Onwards up this steep demanding hill, wild flowers, especially the sunshine-yellow carpet of low-growing birdsfoot trefoil, thrive in the grass, whilst views all around include the Weymouth Bay, Lodmoor Nature Reserve and far inland to Hardy's Monument. This also is an area of erosion, the cliffs slowly but surely slipping away. The area on top was, in the 1930s, a pitch and putt course, but on the death of the then-owner, Mr Arthur Mayne, the land was left to Weymouth Council on condition that the grass be kept short and people allowed to enjoy the area as they pleased. Beside the position of the ninth hole was a wooden hut, where now stands a popular cafe aptly named The Lookout, which remains open throughout the year. A small putting green was once organised around the cafe area, but the rabbits were so busy adding their own holes to the green that the enterprise was eventually abandoned. The original golf course used to continue from the ninth hole, westwards down the hill to end at the eighteenth hole, where close by stood the Nineteenth Cafe, the predecessor of the Embassy (now the Spyglass).

Across the road at the top of the hill many large and expensive (£1 million plus) houses have been built. Apartments have become popular here too — often fetching over half a million pounds. Touring camper-vans used to regularly park along the cliff-top road, abusing the free day and night-time parking spaces, so the local council approved a restriction on overnight parking along the central stretch from 12 pm to 6 am.

From the top of the hill can be seen Fantasy Island Fun Park and the Beachside Leisure Centre, which normally close at the end of October for the season. Beyond these can be seen the crescent-shaped Riviera Hotel. Built in 1937, it bankrupted its original owner. During World War II it was used as accommodation for disabled evacuee children and afterwards became part

of Fred Pontin's holiday park empire. It is a Grade 2 Listed building of special architectural interest, a fine example of Art-Deco. In 2011 it was extended and in 2012 reopened as a three-star hotel offering chalet-style bedrooms, most with views of the beach and Weymouth Bay, two swimming pools, spa facilities and restaurant, open to guests and visitors. It was in this cove that smugglers are said to have landed contraband goods and moved them up the River Jordan to trusted safe areas from which they could be 'delivered to grateful customers'.

Several fields in this valley were originally rented out during the summer months to campers with their tents. In 1963, a local paper reported that these holiday-makers enjoyed the opportunity to come and go as they pleased, free from stern-faced landladies and their strict meal-time regulations. Gradually the tents were replaced with caravans and the site developed further, with modern facilities and comforts.

The history of the Waterside Holiday Park and Spa can be traced back to 1950 when the Jacobs family from London built a shop in the Seaview Caravan Park and later purchased second-hand caravans for letting. In 1963 they bought the Waterside Holiday Park in Bowleaze Cove and relinquished the Seaview shop in order to concentrate fully on their new purchase. Later, the Prebendal Holiday Park nearby was purchased and integrated into the Waterside Holiday Park, this site now having 'a Spa that rivals any 5-star hotel' and 'is regarded as one of the top parks in the country'.

The caravan holiday sites are well organised, maintained and attractively laid out. In November 2006, an appeal by Bourne Leisure against refusal for permission to be granted for 30 extra caravan bases to be placed on one caravan site, and fixed caravans on another, was dismissed by a planning inspector. After listening to strong and determined appeals from local people, he later viewed the area from a distance and stated, 'In my opinion, the swathe of caravans on the existing sites catches the eye of the viewer and their appearance acts as a vivid discordant contrast to the scenic beauty of the outstanding landscape'. Local opposition had won the day.

Passing through the Waterside Holiday Park you reach a gate and footpath from which the local riding school and stables can be seen. Veering left along this delightful but notoriously neglected country lane full of holes and muddy puddles, Church Road and the A353 is finally reached. On the corner is the Spice Ship Inn, originally called the Ship Inn, frequented by sailors and smugglers, with sawdust on the floor and regular cock-fights. Was this name the owner's choice and did it allude to the days when spice was a most valuable commodity? There appears to be no connection with the East India Company or the spice trade.

Originally very small, the inn was later extended through the purchase of adjoining properties. With further modification, what looks like a small inn from the outside now boasts a restaurant area large enough to cater for 65 diners, whilst the open kitchen layout enables those dining to see how their food is prepared. Beyond the dining room is a covered decking area on a nautical theme with large shells, lobster pots and fishing nets, and beyond that a grassy play area for children, together with a flower garden adorned with hanging baskets in the summer. Indoors there is an area for darts and pool, a large TV, and occasional live music and quiz games. There are seven

*The Ship Inn 1924. At one time, locals referred to the area as Ship Corner.*

darts teams, a good and reliable staff and many 'loyal locals'. Interestingly there are two fish and chip shops on either side of the Inn.

# Geology

Situated in an Area of Outstanding Natural Beauty (AONB), the coastline from Bowleaze Cove to Redcliff Point is part of not only the Jurassic Coastline but also England's first World Heritage Site. Short though this stretch of coastline may seem, it can count itself on a par with the Great Barrier Reef and the Grand Canyon, with rocks estimated at around 145 million years old. The main ones here are Oxford Clay and Corallian limestone. The abundant fossils, especially the large oyster Gryphaea, are a good indicator of the Oxford Clay. Corallian limestone is composed of sandstone and limestone and is a pale brownish-orange. Both rocks were deposited as sediment on the sea floor and later, through changes of sea level, exposed as land.

When clay becomes wet and saturated, it loses strength and slumps. Any earth above it sags and the whole section eventually becomes a landslide. Along the east end of the Coveway the beach is composed of pebbles and boulders which, if studied closely, will reveal either fossils or an empty space which might suggest a track, hole or burrow. These empty burrows or holes are known as trace fossils, and this section of the coast is considered as one of the best Jurassic sections on which to study them. Pieces of fossilised wood are often discovered here too, having at some time fallen into the sea, sunk to the bottom and eventually fossilised. Together with fossilised forms of mussels, oysters and cockles, the remains of a crocodile, an elephant and an ichthyosaurus have also been uncovered here. It appears that most of the fossilised creatures once lived either in or on the sea bed, whilst others such as ammonites were free swimming and carried here after death. In 1990 an astonishing find was uncovered here on the beach at low tide, but it was not a fossil; it was a late 9th-century Anglo-Saxon jewel, named later as the Bowleaze Jewel. The find is believed to be an Aestel (a bishop's pointer designed for the reading of manuscripts) and now resides in the British Museum.

*Following an exceptionally wet winter in 2001/02 a serious landslip in this area left the cliffs almost vertical in places, necessitating redirection of the coastal path above and reinforcement of the cliff base below the Riviera Hotel.*

## Roman remains

Between 55 and 54 BC the Romans first invaded Britain, and Roman remains have been found in the area. There must have been a settlement of some importance here, since a Roman villa, temple and cemetery have been uncovered. The site of the villa is shown on OS maps (see map opposite the Introduction and on page 14).

Later, during the second Roman invasion beginning AD 43, Dorchester or

*Engraving of the Roman pavement (from The Illustrated London News 1871) drawn and engraved by the architectural draughtsman and wood-engraver Thomas Sulman to illustrate an article for the Congress of the British Archaeological Association. The article stated that 'At the site of a Roman Villa the pavement tesselated, fresh and perfect as if just laid down.'*

*Durnovaria* became a large Roman military base and Roman remains found on Jordan Hill indicate that it was probably a site set aside for the families of Roman soldiers, sailors and officials who were based in Durnovaria. In 1812 a hoard of several hundred Roman coins was uncovered by some farm labourers ploughing in a field. This find triggered further digs that resulted in unexpected finds and revelations. In 1843–44 the foundation of a Roman temple was discovered, revealing more coins plus fragments of pottery. Late in 1845 several skeletons were unearthed, together with ashes and burnt bones as well as nails and wood probably from coffins. Further excavation in 1930 uncovered bird bones, pottery, a sword and spearhead. The bones

*Remains of the Roman temple found on Jordan Hill.*

of ravens, starlings, crows, buzzards and one hare were discovered in the temple area together with the horns of young bulls, all possibly offered as a form of sacrifice and ritual to the gods. It is interesting that the descendants of the birds are still seen today in the same area. Rabbits and deer can also be seen on Jordan Hill, but there is no mention of either from the Roman era (though rabbits are known to have been introduced to this country by the Romans).

Pottery was also discovered amongst the finds, thought to have been made by the local Durotriges tribe, a Celtic clan that were probably the inhabitants who settled on Chalbury Hill centuries before the Romans arrived. It has been surmised that the Romans and descendants of the Durotriges may have shared the temple and cemetery facilities in an amicable relationship, since items relating to both groups and their individual rituals have been uncovered together during some excavations. Jordan Hill remains still a site of archaeological interest for there is a possibility that further excavation may reveal additional items and a greater knowledge of past events. It is understood that whilst pottery and coins have been removed from the Roman site, skeletal remains have been carefully and sensitively replaced.

In 1930, a housing development was proposed on Jordan Hill by Weymouth Bay Estate Co. In 1933, plots with a 55-ft frontage and 200-ft depth were

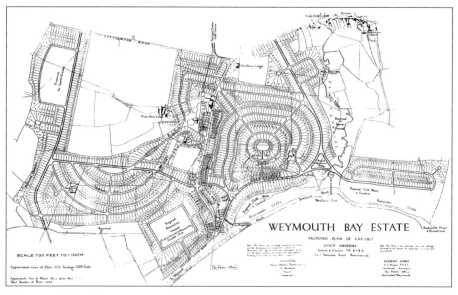

*Weymouth Bay Estate proposed plan of layout, showing 1333 plots. (To view a larger version of this plan go to www.rovingpress.co.uk.)*

offered for sale but only a few were purchased. The estate was planned to spread from Overcombe Cliffs across the hill to Littlemoor Road, east to the River Jordan and west towards Weymouth. It was to include a sports ground off Littlemoor Road, a recreation ground for Weymouth Cricket Club, a sports field along the banks of the River Jordan and ornamental gardens in Bowleaze Cove. A few plots were sold but a local action group rose to challenge this proposed unwanted development. Door-to-door visits gathered sufficient money to obtain the advice of an eminent barrister and when the council, through a local survey, estimated the total cost to build such an estate as too expensive, the plan was finally discarded.

## *Preston's nonagenarian*

In Wales in 1917, a year before World War I ended, Ron Price was born. Ninety-five years or more later he is here in Preston, still lively, active, independent and blessed with a delightful sense of humour and a joy for living – a truly remarkable man.

The only child of loving, caring parents, he lived with them in South Wales in a coal-mining valley where accidents in the pits were frequent and disastrous, so much so that his father was concerned for his son's future and pondered deeply on this. Whilst on a day trip to Weymouth, a good friend noticed a shop for sale on Bowleaze Corner and, when he returned home, spoke to Mr Price about it. Without delay, Mr and Mrs Price, together with their son, took a train to Weymouth and from there walked to Overcombe Corner to investigate the property themselves.

Captivated immediately, Mr Price realised not only the shop's potential but also the area's enchantment as a place to live, so close to the sea and not a coal mine in sight! Rushing home, he contacted a firm of valuers who took 2 days to assess the situation, reminding him of the possible financial complications since the summer might be busy but in winter when short of visitors they would be on low income. Undeterred, Mr Price knew in his heart that this was meant to be. He was quick to appreciate that with accurate judgement of the commodities required by local people, the business could succeed. The family had high standards, worked hard and thrived, adding to their property as each opportunity arose. When retirement eventually came in 1957, they sold their shop to the Joy family who have been there ever since.

*The General Stores in 1936.*

# Chapter 5
# Overcombe to Chalbury Corner

On the left entering Preston Road is a group of businesses, the first and most long-standing being Joy's, the newsagent, shop and post office. In 2007, having been in business for 50 years, Mr and Mrs Joy celebrated their Golden Anniversary. Before the Joy family took over, the shop was but a small area on the ground floor where sweets, tobacco and newspapers were sold, and from which deliveries were made around the area. Stock was also for sale outside in the summer, and two cigarette machines lit up at night for outside opening hours stood on the forecourt. A post office was added in 1960 and, with new houses being built in the area, the shop began to expand. Since then, both shop and home have been extended and modernised. The owners are respected throughout the neighbourhood for their reliable service, well-maintained and varied stock and the care they take to satisfy customers' needs.

Next to Joy's is DOMVS, an estate agency with offices in both Preston and Dorchester. The business is well established and through the Preston branch offers a wide selection of local properties, many with views of the

Dorset coastline. In 2008 they launched a Lettings division, offering a full property maintenance and lettings service. It is interesting to note here that the Latin alphabet has 23 letters as opposed to 26 in the English alphabet, the three missing letters being j, v and w. *Collins' General Latin Dictionary* explains that 'the symbol v was the capital form of the letter u, but in a later age the small v came into use to represent the consonant u'. The word *domus* in Latin is written in lower case and translates as 'house, especially in a town'. DOMVS, the estate agency, has its name in capital letters, hence the V instead of a U but sounded as 'u'.

Further along is a florist's shop delightfully named Pogles Wood. Bouquets, sprays and baskets of flowers, both fresh and artificial, are created here for special occasions, and as well as local flowers, others are purchased from Holland and Columbia. Overseas orders from servicemen and women and relatives and friends in Australia and New Zealand are dealt with via the Internet and delivered by Interflora.

Apart from South Down Cottage and Jordan Farm, a 1903 map shows no dwellings in place along the road from Overcombe Corner to Chalbury Corner. However, a later 1937 map reveals that, over the intervening years a great change had taken place, with at least thirty detached and individually designed homes set in large gardens well established along the road. Today, several of these houses have been sold and demolished, with apartments built in their stead that have proved popular with retired people.

Built of brick and stone, and with a slated not a thatched roof, South Down Cottage stood close to the road surrounded by trees and fields. Its position can be seen on the 1937 OS map of the area. On the ground floor, in addition to the usual downstairs facilities, it boasted a conservatory, butler's pantry, wine cellar and housekeeper's room. There were five bedrooms on the first floor, together with a bathroom, hot and cold water and WC. On the second floor there was another bedroom plus a box room and heated linen cupboards. Water was on tap and there was a cess pool for drainage. Outside, together with a kitchen garden, there was a small paddock and tennis lawns.

Here the two Miss Norris sisters lived until, sadly, the property had to be sold in order to pay death duties. All that remains today is the spinney, which the two sisters were adamant should be left for local children to enjoy. On the land that once extended beyond South Down Cottage, neat bungalows, apartments and houses were built and the roads named after local trees, such as Hazel Down, Pinemoor Close, Cherry Way, Ash Way, Oak Way, Elm Close and Orchard Drive.

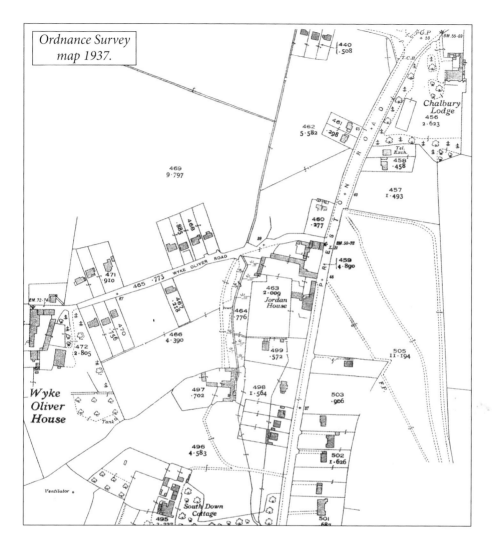

Ordnance Survey map 1937.

This part of Preston Road is lined with a variety of trees that add pleasure and character to the area. One is a very large horse chestnut tree which flowers each year with a riot of blossom in spring and a host of conkers in autumn. Part of the Latin name for the horse chestnut tree is *hippocastanum* (*hippo* meaning horse and *castanum* meaning chestnut). It got its name because chestnuts in Turkey were once used as a source of food and medicine for horses; they were also eaten by cattle and deer, and sometimes ground up as a fattening food for sheep. Today, they are still recommended as a deterrent for moths instead of moth balls. In Britain the seeds are known as 'conkers', which is short for 'conquerors'. The game of conkers was originally played with snail shells and cob nuts, the former often with the snail still inside.

A little further along the road is Jordan House which was built *c* 1800 and

faces south. It was here that Dr Sloan, assisted by Dr Temple, set up a small surgery. Today, Preston has a modern surgery which was built on a strip of land once part of Chalbury House estate. This practice has a group of dedicated male and female doctors, together with specialist nurses and secretarial staff, and holds both morning and evening surgeries.

*Jordan House still has its original fan-light design over the front door and sash windows each side.*

The roundabout at Chalbury Corner is regularly maintained with flower beds set around a sturdy palm tree donated by a local business. On the green adjacent at sporadic intervals throughout the year a local fisherman sells freshly caught fish from his van, whilst at Christmas a large tree, courtesy of Goadsby estate agents, is erected and entwined with fairy lights, around which folk gather to sing carols.

Chalbury Lodge, near the roundabout, was built in 1840 in Regency style but considerably altered *c* 1934. On the death of the owner it was destined to be converted into a home for the elderly, but the transaction failed and the land was used instead for a small housing estate. A ghost is said to appear occasionally, walking from Chalbury House along the driveway and disappearing into the dark, wearing pyjamas and cap, yet no one knows who he was or the background to his jaunts.

# Chapter 6
# Chalbury Corner to Seven Acres

Heading from Chalbury Corner towards a bus shelter and in the direction of Sutton Poyntz, a narrow and almost hidden footpath can be found on the right running parallel with a low hedge that separates it from Preston Road. A 1903 OS map indicates this side of the road as boggy, and as such so it remains today. Around 1930, on the opposite side of the road, the land was being divided into plots and sold privately for housing development. As an example of the price and details of these houses, an original document reveals information relating to plot No. 620 which was estimated at £1225. The property contained a front room, dining room, bathroom and upstairs WC, with one external WC and some offices. Drainage was 'strictly in accordance with the Local Bye laws, and a Cesspool with filter bed provided to receive the sewage'.

The A353 now carries heavy traffic. There is a pedestrian crossing near the Weymouth Bay Holiday Park and one near the Village Hall across to the SPAR shop; the latter replaced a small island set midway across the road after a lad from the caravan site was killed when endeavouring to reach the other side. In 2010 two traffic speed cameras were installed along the same road.

Both the SPAR shop and internal Post Office are well used by the community. The Clements family run the shop today and before that it was the Baileys. The Bailey family was known and respected in the area and Stan Bailey, together with his widowed mother, ran their own shop along Preston Road. When she died, he built a new shop which, on his eventual retirement, was bought freehold by the Clements family who also purchased the local post office and moved it into their shop, where it stands today. The name 'Bailey' was removed from the store and replaced with SPAR, an international company which offers shop owners a chance to remain independent whilst using SPAR as a wholesaler.

In 1944 an appeal was started to erect a village hall as a 'Memorial of Gratitude' to the local women for the part they played in World War II. Many years later, in 1962, the hall was completed, with the adjacent Weymouth Bay Holiday Park donating an area for car parking. As time passed various extensions were added to the Hall, including the stage, worked on by prisoners from the Verne on Portland.

Amongst its main uses now are pre-school preparation classes, dancing (ballroom and line-dancing) and fitness groups. Amateur dramatics and the annual pantomime are a local 'must' for residents who appreciate not only the acting but also the scenery, costumes and amount of work entailed. The occasional 'gaffe' adds to their delight and laughter.

It was as far back as 1979 that the local pantomimes began, the first production being *Robinson Crusoe* presented in the Scutt Memorial Hall in Sutton Road. This was the beginning of a local tradition which is as strong today as it was then. Apart from *Aladdin* and *Mother Goose*, which were presented in the Riviera in 1984 and 1985 respectively, and a few more in the Scutt Hall, the rest have been produced in the Village Hall.

In 1986 the children of the adult pantomime group formed their own group – Preston Pantomime Kids (PPK). Together with interested friends, these young people, aged between 10 and 15, meet on Friday evenings to learn and enjoy acting. There is fun and laughter both on the stage and in the audience as PPK present their own pantomime to the public. This training hopefully provides further talent for the adult group later on, and also develops within the young people a measure of self-confidence and concentration.

A few doors down from the SPAR shop is 'Chic' Hairdressing and Beauty Salon, which was once a hairdresser's salon upstairs and a wool shop at ground level. Today's owner amused her parents when, in her teens, she declared quite seriously that she wished to own and run a salon of her own when she grew up. Her determination remained and after several years of serious study and practice, she moved from a salon on the Dorchester Road in May 2003 to Preston. Here, together with facials, manicures and massage, she has built up her clientele and business.

Further down, on the corner of Seven Acres Road, once stood a garage and house owned by Mr Chappell. Although known locally as somewhat of a recluse, he was a pleasant and helpful man who could 'repair anything'. The garage, said to contain every appropriate and available tool, was described as an Aladdin's cave, full of car and motorcycle bits, and with a petrol pump on the forecourt. Both house and garage were eventually demolished and replaced with a small block of flats known as Whitelee Court.

The only garage left in the vicinity of Preston today is the White Horse Garage found along the road to Osmington and with a magnificent view across the bay. Once a petrol station, it is now split into two separately owned businesses – a car sales lot and Top Gear, which deals with everything else including vehicle repairs, maintenance and MOTs. The Garage is so named because a White Horse can be clearly seen on the hillside inland, carved in 1808 as a gesture of respect to King George III who had a great affection for Weymouth and spent many holidays there during his reign.

Returning now to Seven Acres Road, there are, on the right and up the hill, several dwellings and cottages and a small cul-de-sac named Rymbury. From here it is just possible to see Rimbrow Coppice, on a small hill south-east of Chalbury Hill. Funeral urns and burnt boxes were discovered here, suggesting the site was a necropolis or ancient burial ground for the Stone Age inhabitants on Chalbury Hill.

On the opposite side of Seven Acres Road, a Roman Catholic church once stood, but due to lack of attendance it was demolished in the late 1970s and houses erected in its place. Prior to this, the entire area from Brunel Drive to Coombe Valley was farmland covering approximately 7 acres (2.8 ha), hence the name of Seven Acres Road. The land rapidly became a housing estate in the 1960s, the dwellings a variety of designs erected by different builders. Along Stanier Road productive orchards were cut down in order to erect more homes, which saddened many locals.

Ernie Coleman began development of the estate, starting at Rhosewood Drive, with homes ready for occupation in 1963. The houses opposite were finished shortly afterwards. At the same time Wainwright Close and Churchward Avenue were also being developed, each dwelling again individually designed. Mr Coleman was a railway enthusiast, hence the naming of roads after railway engineers (for instance, Telford, Maunsell, Stanier and Hawksworth). Housing was critical at this time since homes were required for naval officers, scientists and research experts who, brought in to work at Winfrith Nuclear Research Centre, the Ministry of Defence on Portland and the Research Establishment at Bincleaves, required accommodation for themselves and their families.

Each Christmas, on the corner of Seven Acres Road and Brunel Drive, a magnificent Christmas display is laid out in a private front garden. Families going to and from school gaze enthralled by its magic. Closer to Christmas a carol service accompanied by the Salvation Army Band has been held around the garden. The philosophy behind this enchanting display originates not only from the dedicated lady designer's childhood delight in the legend of Santa Claus but also in the Christian aspect of the season.

# Chapter 7
# Telford Recreation Park

Telford Park off Telford Close was once a field the bottom of which was regularly boggy and where an old and dilapidated pavilion and football pitch existed for several years. The children's play area has not always been there but is now fenced off so that little children can play safely, leaving the open space for older youngsters.

The grass across the field in earlier days was not kept as short and trim as it is today, and local people appreciate and value this care. In earlier times, the entrance was through a hole in the fence at the end of Stanier Road, with the field used for dog walking. It was also the scene for the occasional bonfire and firework night and even a Donkey Derby. At one stage it was under consideration as a site for the new St Andrew's C.E. primary school, but the area was too small and a larger site was eventually found on Littlemoor Road. On one occasion, as a retirement honour, a naval officer from Portland was flown home to Preston in a helicopter which landed on the field, and once an Air Ambulance helicopter put down here in an emergency.

Over the years dog owners have met and formed friendships. With the guidance and support of the local councillor, they formed a small but enterprising group with its own committee and finances to help look after the Park. With one seat already in the Park, it was decided, on the demise of a respected, popular and supportive member, John Willis, to add a second seat and commemorative plaque in his memory. The council, when consulted, surprised by the dedication of the group and its care and thoughtfulness regarding the Park and children's play area, helped physically and financially

*Cindy in Telford Park. This energetic and much-loved dog is often seen racing across the field, catching a ball in mid-air.*

with the installation of two new seats, a notice board and metal gate. Telford Recreation Park may only be a small field but it is well used, cared for and, above all, enjoyed.

# Preston footballers

Football today is no longer the prerogative of men and boys but is also seriously enjoyed by girls and women. Boys and girls can be seen playing football amicably together in the park, and some are members of the school and local teams, with one girl already selected to play for the Dorset Under 12 Girls' Team.

In 1966 a group of young men formed themselves into a football club and carried out their training not only in the summer months but also under floodlight in the winter. Their football ground was at the back of Preston Road where a club house was erected on land now developed with housing. The team's colours were red and black-striped shirts and black shorts, and when they entered the Dorset League Division IV South and West in 1966 they earned themselves a good reputation by winning every game. In 1967 they were able to form a reserve team to enter Division IV as the first team had succeeded in promotion to Division III South and West.

*First Team members Syd Bateman, Tim Squib, Dickie Drew, Lennie Harris, Graham Wilkinson, David Lake, John Barrow, Tony Taylor, Doug Clarke, Les Lusted (Captain) and Jimmy Hoskins. Jack Jollife was team trainer, the Chairman was Laurie G. Barrow, Treasurer Clive Townsend and Hon Sec Richard (Dick) Gaunt. Other team members included Graham Mullins, Tony Hornsby, Malcolm Harris, Dave Barrow, Chris Galpin and Keith Little.*

# Chapter 8
## Littlemoor Road

Back in 1937 a local map shows no businesses at the start of Littlemoor Road, whereas today there are six businesses around this small green. One named Chalbury Stores selling hardware, alcohol and pet food was taken over in 2004 and renamed the Chalbury Wine Store. Closed for several months for reorganisation, it reopened as an off-licence and newsagent and by Easter 2011 had added a delicatessen to the enterprise. Next to the Wine Store is Formotion Clinics, which offers physiotherapy, chiropody/podiatry, massage, osteopathy and medical acupuncture.

Head Style, the hairdressing salon, opened in 1990. Its popular and well-respected proprietress has been dressing hair there for over 20 years, having built up a faithful clientele not only from Preston but also from Portland, Dorchester and Crossways. Head Style is a family concern with three generations involved as well as two assistants trained and competent in various styles and cuts.

The present pharmacy is thought originally to have been a grocery shop. It changed use in 1964 when John Hardy served as pharmacist for 14 years, followed in 1978 by Ken Heathfield who remained for 25 years, before David Norsworthy took it over in 2003. In 2006 it changed to Rowland's Pharmacy and has been redesigned internally with a shop area where customers can select their purchases themselves, the pharmacy set separately on one side. Conveniently sited close to the local surgery, the pharmacist and shop assistants are kept busy.

Goadsby next door was originally called Adam, Rench and Wright, but, with later updating, it was renamed Goadsby and Harding. Rarely, however, was the name Harding used except on paper, and the firm's title is now reduced to simply Goadsby. The business was established in Bournemouth in 1958, with expansion undertaken in the 1970s. With the invention of the computer, so much information can now be stored and manipulated, resulting in the 20 secretaries originally required in the Bournemouth branch being dispensed with and in Preston the post of secretary changing to Assistant Manager. In spite of challenging recessions in the 1980s and early 1990s, the business has remained, the Preston branch receiving praise and recognition from the company for its prowess.

The final business, a fencing and decking contractors, can be seen across the Littlemoor Road opposite the green. It has a range of wooden sheds attractively laid out across the well-trimmed grass amongst a delightful and amusing array of garden ornaments and statues.

The Littlemoor Road is aptly named since it runs from Chalbury Corner to Littlemoor. For a short distance on either side of the road there is a stretch of attractive and individually designed houses, some with interesting names such as The Doll's House, The Old Vicarage, Mount Laurel and Sweet Briar. Immediately beyond the housing is the main entrance to St Andrew's C.E. School and Westfield Arts College, with crossing wardens on regular duty during term time. Beyond the housing and education establishments are several businesses including West Dorset Aquatics, Larkin's Conservatory Village, Gould's Garden Centre, a dog groomer and PamPurred Pets.

Apart from also being a local bus route, Littlemoor Road became an even busier road after the new Weymouth Relief Road had been completed and was faster, safer and more direct than the route across the ridge and down Coombe Valley Road.

## Westfield Arts College

Westfield Arts College along the Littlemoor Road was opened in March 1976 as an educational establishment for children who have moderate learning difficulties and require special educational provision. In the past the

*An early aerial view of St Andrew's School and Westfield Arts College.*

school was a specialist technology college, but in September 2010 it changed to specialise in Visual and Performing Arts. There are 188 pupils on the present role and 140 staff, a percentage of whom are support staff assisting the children in the classroom. One third of these children are diagnosed as having an Autistic Spectrum Disorder (ASD) and require a different approach to learning from those in mainstream schools. Nevertheless, they undertake the full National Curriculum plus a wide range of extra-curricular activities.

In the spring of 2011, a new community radio station, AIR, was launched by Westfield Arts College where pupils operate and broadcast the system themselves. All classes are involved in the radio station, with some children, normally uncommunicative, tackling this new venture with interest, confidence and enthusiasm. The school offers a pleasant, caring and lively atmosphere, together with an aura of complete dedication and understanding from both education and administrative staff. A series of support programmes is also in place for parents.

# Chapter 9
# Coombe Valley

Coombe Valley runs from Littlemoor Road up to the South Dorset Ridgeway where, in 1929, the only habitation along what was a winding country lane were two farms, with one gate somewhere across the bottom of the road and a second gate near the spring known as Boiling Rock (at the end of the later housing development, on the right). In 1797 an Act of Parliament granted the taking of water from Boiling Rock to add to Weymouth's water supply.

*The road in flood one bad winter after heavy storms.*

At the foot of the hill stood Coombe Barton Farm with a sheep wash and spring. Nearby and opposite the farm, a track crossed the stream and ran uphill to a poultry farm, where the primary school stands today. Further along, near the junction with the road to Sutton Poyntz, stood Green Barton Farm, the ruins of which are still visible. An attempt several years ago was made to rebuild there in the hope that tenants or holiday-makers could be accommodated. However, permission was not forthcoming and the scheme fell through. Sadly, the site itself and the caravan used by the potential developer were left neglected and derelict.

In 1937 the OS map records three residences on and just past the turn-off from Littlemoor Road as far as Coombe Barton Farm, and further along on the right just past what is now Rhosewood Drive, detached houses were built with long gardens at the front and some with gardens at the rear rising steeply up the hill behind. Later development saw similar dwellings on both sides of the road.

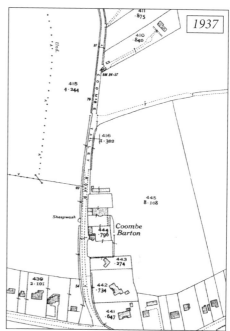

It was in this valley during World War II that a damaged German aircraft crash-landed and set fire to a dwelling. One story tells how local folk dashed to see the wrecked aircraft, quietly removing from it small items as mementos. For a while during the war, two old railway carriages in Coombe Valley housed six people made homeless through a bombing raid, four in one and two in the other. There were no 'mod-cons', just oil lamps, a bucket as an outdoor toilet, and water from an animal trough supplied from a single water tap. Peggy Simpson of Oaklands Park, Warmwell, together with her sisters and step-father Ted Bray lived in one of the carriages.

Limestone quarries along the valley have been a source of good building material over the years, with this area mentioned in the 14th century as 'the locality whence the stone was exported to London'. 'Exported' may seem a strange word to use but in those days stone was shipped along the coast and up the Thames to London, since there were no juggernauts to convey it then by

51

road as they do today. It is said that lumps of stone gathered from this quarry were deposited in Lodmoor waters as Billy Butlin endeavoured to build the foundations needed to establish a holiday camp there. The quarry area is used frequently nowadays by young enthusiasts practising and extending their scrambling skills on mountain bikes and motor cycles.

Above the quarry and accessible from it is Chalbury Hill, recorded on a 1903 OS map as *Chalbury Camp* with two tumuli, or burial mounds, on top. As far back as AD 946 Chalbury Hill was recorded as *Cheoles burge*, *Cheol* possibly being the name of a Saxon chieftain and *burge* the Old English for *burh* or *burg* meaning a shelter or dwelling place for a specific clan or a tribal heritage.

*Even today there are clear traces of a well-organised settlement on Chalbury Hill, with but one entrance in the defensive embankment and a clear view across both land and sea where approaching invaders could be spotted and prepared for.*

Somewhere in the vicinity two female ghosts are reputed to appear occasionally. One is that of a pregnant, unmarried servant girl, who was turned out by her mistress into the snow on Christmas Eve and never seen again alive. Another is that of a suicide; having been insolent to gypsies camped by an old tree at the head of the valley east of Came Wood (OS grid ref. SY699855) called the Culliford Tree, she had a terrifying gypsy curse cast upon her and afterwards committed suicide.

The tree has an interesting history. It grows atop an important local

barrow which over the ages has been found to contain cremations, Bronze Age pottery and medieval inhumations. It was used as a moot or ancient meeting place for the local 'Hundred' , a word that derives from a banding together of men or homesteads for protection. Each Hundred was presided over by a Reeve, who was responsible for the overall management of the village on behalf of the king. Regular meetings were held at some prominent local feature, hence the Culliford Tree on the ridge. The Reeves from each settlement would have represented their villages and when young boys reached the age of 12, they would have been taken along to formally swear an oath of loyalty to their king.

In the early 1970s Coombe Valley Road, once a winding, picturesque country lane, was used by local families for quiet, relaxing Sunday walks

with their children who were either walking too or on their bicycles. Gradually, however, as the density of traffic increased, it was slowly dominated by drivers wishing to avoid traffic congestion on the A354 between Dorchester and Weymouth. In 2011, with the completion of the Weymouth Relief Road, the density of vehicles on this road has gradually eased, though perhaps not sufficient to return it to the quiet country lane it once was.

Coombe Valley Road is a plant-lover's delight throughout the year. For those with both interest and keen eyesight, it is possible occasionally to find an orchid or two amongst the grass along the high roadside verge. Although common on the Continent, the spring snowflake was introduced into Britain as a garden plant but, over the years, it has become naturalised and is now described as 'very rare in damp scrub and hedge banks in Dorset and Somerset'. Between February and March a few specimens flower beside the stream where Coombe Valley Road straightens out. It resembles the common snowdrop but differs in that it is approximately twice the snowdrop's height and usually flowers later, with each flower-head bearing six distinctive green-tipped white petals. Pyracantha or 'Firethorn' is a magnificent shrub with its fiery coloured berries and thorny shoots. A member of the Olive family, lilac displays its mauve flowers in delicate clusters during May. Laburnum, or 'Golden Chain', in spite of its glorious colouring, is one of the most poisonous trees found in Britain. Introduced from central Europe around the 16th century, its clusters of hanging yellow flowers attract pollinating insects. Weeping Willows are also a joy to behold, and beyond the housing hawthorn and gorse add their colouring to spring's pageantry.

'Mind-your own business' can also be seen. Its small pink flowers bloom between May and October whilst its myriad of miniature leaves form green cushions alongside stream edges either side of the road. Its alternative names of 'Baby's Tears' and 'Paddy's Wig' appropriately describe the tiny leaves, but its third nomenclature, 'Mind Your Own Business', remains a mystery.

The Monterey pine can be found wild in a small area of California, its native home. It will, however, grow well in southern England. Cones can be seen on the tree throughout most of the year.

Weeping willow will hybridise freely with one another. They are fast-growing trees and were some of the earliest trees to recolonise after the Ice Age in Britain.

# Chapter 10
# Wyke Oliver Road

At the turn of the 19th century there were several farms in Preston including Preston Farm, Jordon Farm, South Downs Dairy, Manor Farm, Coombe Barton, Green Barton and Wyke Oliver, the latter at the far end of Wyke Oliver Road. *Wyke* means farm and this farm was probably lived in originally by a family called Oliver. Henry Legg and family moved here in 1933. Henry was succeeded by his son Richard, and on now to a third generation which continues farming here.

Over the years the farm has seen many changes not only in agriculture but in its surroundings too. Sadly, in the 1970s, Wyke Oliver House situated nearby was demolished and a large estate built which eventually blocked the Legg family's view across the fields to the main road and beyond. What was once their vegetable garden now has three houses in it, and they would no longer dare take their bull across the Preston Road to a field of cows beyond. Cows from Jordon Farm were also herded daily along the same road from their pasture to the milking parlour – just imagine the chaos that would cause today!

*Wyke Oliver Road 1967.*

*Wyke Oliver Farm today with its pigs, goats, free-range chickens, ducks, bantams, geese and quail, products of which are all available for purchase locally in season.*

Almost opposite Oakbury Drive is Macpherson House, a property owned by Abbeyfield (Weymouth) Society Ltd. Whilst this is a home for the elderly, it is not a 'care' home but a 'caring' home for those who are still reasonably independent but prefer not to live alone. Each occupant has his or her own en-suite self-furnished room which is cleaned weekly. There is a communal utility room where occupants can deal with their own laundry, and they are supplied with provisions to make their own breakfast. Hot lunches and evening meals are cooked daily, and relatives and friends are free to visit.

Oakbury Drive Spinney once belonged to South Down Cottage. This small but precious woodland area has been carefully and sensitively restored, managed and fenced. There are two gates, one of which remains unlocked and offers entry to passers-by interested enough to make a brief diversion and enjoy this woodland sanctuary with its wild flowers, mature trees, fungi, lichens, birds and the occasional small deer. For such a small spinney situated

in a built-up area, this tiny patch of woodland yields an interesting selection of wild flowers both in quantity and variety. In 2008 a sample study revealed 31 families of flowers and 88 different species.

Oakbury Drive runs from Wyke Oliver Road towards Lodmoor. A rough footpath leads into Lodmoor, and where it turns sharp left, on the right can be seen a grassy hill on which there is a line of trees. This is Horse Lynch

Plantation. Here in December 2001 a character named 'Swampy' (Daniel Hooper, a well-known national environmental activist) together with companions camped out, dedicated in their protest against the destruction of beautiful countryside by the proposed relief road planned to ease the increasing traffic congestion along the Dorchester Road. For a few weeks they were the focal point for television and newspaper headlines until eventually the proposal was dismissed and all went quiet. Nevertheless, several years later, after Weymouth was selected to host the 2012 Olympic Sailing Competition, the by-pass was finally agreed with promises that 'the beautiful countryside' through which it had intruded would be sympathetically landscaped with trees and shrubs appropriate to the terrain.

# Chapter II

# Lodmoor

Lodmoor Nature Reserve completes our tour of Preston. In the 12th century the name was recorded as *Lotmoor* and in 1284 as *Loddemore*, which translates appropriately as 'swampy ground', *lut* or *lot* being Old English for mud. For some time it appeared difficult to decide what to do with Lodmoor and its seemingly useless land, but what a blessing it was that Billy Butlin was eventually denied the opportunity to build a holiday camp there, for Lodmoor is now fully appreciated as a valuable and popular nature reserve and RSPB site. It is open at all times, tracks offering easy access along firm, flat and wide paths, suitable for cyclists, pushchairs and invalid carriages. There are occasional organised wildlife walks for both local visitors and dedicated ornithologists from this country and abroad.

Japanese knotweed, the overpowering plant that has grown and spread vigorously around the reserve and nationally, was choking all within in its vicinity. It provided neither cover nor food for native birds and insects, and soon dominated all surrounding vegetation. Notices in 2011 around the reserve clearly explained the reason for the drastic operation regarding its destruction. After being cut down in late summer the hollow stems that were left were filled with herbicide, thus causing no harm to surrounding vegetation. This method of killing the roots has been proven successful by the National Trust in conjunction with Exeter University.

The reserve has open water and grazing marshes, reed beds, trees, shrubs and small shallow pools. Reeds dominate Lodmoor, creating extensive beds of long, creeping and tangled networks of roots that form over the mud and, once established, are difficult to remove. These reed beds provide many water birds with nesting sites, feeding ground and good cover at breeding time. Entering the reserve from the end of Southdown Avenue leads the walker past the first reed beds, with yellow iris a bright contrast to the rustling reeds in spring and summer. On around the corner, the reeds provide sheltered territory for moorhens and coots. Moorhens are small and dark with a white line along each side of the body and white under the tail; the bill is red with a yellow tip. Coots are a similar size and colour but have a white bill and forehead. One clear difference between them is that, unlike most water birds, the moorhen does not have webbed feet.

Moving on and turning left again it is possible to find flowers of all types, including hemlock water dropwort. This tall, hairless, white flower has grooved stems, is parsley scented and very poisonous. Here too sometimes is a swan's nest, large, shallow and untidy. Along this same track there once stood a well-used hide until vandals burned it down. Close to here you may see a spoonbill; this is a rare vagrant similar to a large white heron but with

a long black bill that ends in a yellow spoon shape. The swans at Lodmoor are mute swans with orange bills, the female (pen) laying 5–8 pale greenish-white eggs which are guarded by both male (cob) and female.

On again is a clear and safely guarded stretch with hand rails and a place from which food can be thrown to the cluster of gregarious mallards in residence here. This is shallow water and a favourite spot for mallards but more humorous for bird-watchers in winter when the water may be frozen and the mallards can be seen to slither across the ice, unbalanced like drunkards. Close by here, tiny dunnocks or hedge-sparrows hop nervously along the ground near to cover, constantly flicking their wings as they seek food under the bushes.

Two small pebbled islands have been set up especially for the host of noisy common terns that arrive in spring for breeding. The colony at Lodmoor is one of the largest breeding groups in the south-west and special man-made islands keep them flocking in. Their nests are a mere scrape, and their noisy screams echo as they rise in a frantic whirling flight across the water, wildly chasing any of their brethren carrying a freshly caught fish in its beak. The sea, just a short flight away across Preston Beach Road, is their feeding ground. At this point along the route, a Cetti's warbler may be detected, its presence highlighted by its explosive, scolding cry. It is a skulking bird and another 'little brown job', but from just one known pair in 1998, they have now spread around the reserve.

Left again around the next corner are several tall white poplar trees. The underside of their leaves is white-felted, hence its name of white poplar; these hairs protect the leaf's breathing pores from becoming clogged with salt particles and pollution.

Further along this stretch is an attractive open-fronted shelter which was a replacement for another vandalised hide. From here there is a clear view across the reserve and a chance to enjoy the swifts and swallows in summer as they swerve above. You may also see a heron quietly still or slowly moving, intensely focused on the water as it hunts for prey. It will also eat water voles, moles and eels as well as fish, and is a delight to watch. Little egrets and peregrine falcons are sometimes visitors to the area, and the list of winter visitors includes wigeon, gadwall, teal, shoveller, tufted duck, pochards and lapwings. There is no doubt that binoculars are a 'must' on Lodmoor!

Not far from the hide is an area dense with teasels. It is possible to find common spotted, pyramidal and bee orchids, the latter so-named since part of it resembles the rear of a small bumble bee visiting the flower; this is thought to be a trick of Nature to attract the male bee to the flower in order to pollinate it. Around this area you may also spot a kingfisher, and deer have been seen, running through the water.

The circuit around Preston is now complete, for Preston Beach Road runs along the edge of Lodmoor close to where the Toll Gate once stood and the journey around Preston began.

*Bee orchids (left) flower from late May to July. Pyramidal (middle) and common spotted orchids (right) both like to grow in dry, lime and grassy places. Common spotted are the most successful orchid colonisers of waste land. (Pyramidal orchid courtesy of Ian Capper.)*

# Chapter 12
# Round and About Preston

## Local weather

Preston is situated in a dip between the cliffs along the coast and the South Dorset Ridgeway. It nestles in a hollow and consequently has its own micro-climate; at times, when the sun shines here, there is rain just over the ridge in Dorchester and vice versa. Yet it is not precluded from bad weather. In 1950 it rained so heavily and prolonged that several caravans were washed into the river and fairground stalls out to sea. Again, in July 1955, 11 inches (28 cm) of rain fell overnight.

During the winter of 1962/63 snow fell so deep that a photograph recorded a snowdrift that reached at least three-quarters of the way up a lamp-post. Icicles up to 6 inches in length hung everywhere and with no central heating or electric fires the windows froze over inside and out. Every road was impassable, preventing deliveries of food, papers and mail. Sick patients could not be reached by nurse or doctor, school attendance was cancelled and water pipes froze and split; helicopters dropped bales of hay for stranded animals, and fish are said to have died in the sea.

Driven by a forceful wind that lasted several hours, a second blizzard in February 1978 buried Preston and much of Dorset in deep snowdrifts. Villages were isolated for several weeks, with some folk rescued by naval helicopter or tractor. Later, in June 1983, gale force winds, under a dark and lowering sky, drove hail stones the size of golf balls across the land, the torrential rain that followed flooding both Coombe Valley and Preston Beach Road, thus rendering both roads impassable.

In June 1983, 2 inches of rain fell in about an hour in Coombe Valley Road, filling the ditches to overflowing and causing a swirling stream across the

road. A third bad winter in December 2010 brought Preston to yet another standstill. The snow was not unusually deep but severe night frosts caused treacherous roads, drives and pavements, with only the A353 gritted and open. Cars and vans were unable to negotiate the side roads, the schools were closed and only a few people reached their work. The local No. 4 and 4B buses to Preston and Sutton Poyntz were cancelled since the steep hills en route were too treacherous to negotiate. Many folk during this disrupted period had cause to thank some kind soul who thoughtfully etched in large letters in the snow at the Chalbury Corner bus stop NO BUSES TODAY!

## *Police matters*

In earlier times, around the beginning of the 19th century when the village comprised little more than Preston Street stretching from the church to the River Jordan, the local policeman lived in a house in Preston Street amongst the community where he knew everyone and they knew him. Today Preston covers a far more extensive area and has what is now termed a PCSO (Police Community Support Officer). The following extract from the Dorset Police website describes their work:

> The primary role of a PCSO in Dorset is to contribute to the policing of neighbourhoods, primarily through highly visible uniformed cycle or foot patrol, with the purpose of engaging and reassuring the public, increasing orderliness

in public places and being accessible to communities and partner agencies, through joint working at local level. In carrying out this role, PCSOs support the delivery of a force's strategic aims of ensuring that our communities are listened to, understood, informed, protected and safe.

In 2010 a spate of house burglaries, together with stolen or deliberately scratched cars, took place in Preston, with one group of offenders fortunately and quickly tracked down and arrested on a caravan site as they dismantled a stolen vehicle. One lady had her handbag stolen from her unlocked side kitchen door, and another instance occurred when a house that had been burgled was burgled again immediately after replacement items had been purchased and installed. Advice offered by the police indicated that more community contact was needed, not necessarily implying that neighbours should be 'best friends' but that they should keep a close watch on each other's property, especially when they knew someone was away from home.

## The Ridgeway

*The Ridgeway* church magazine is published by the Team Rector and covers St Andrew's, Preston; Holy Trinity, Bincombe; St Nicholas, Broadwey; St Nicholas, Buckland Ripers; St Francis, Littlemoor; St Osmund, Osmington; and St Laurence, Upwey. It exists 'to share Church stories of encouragement, history, frustration, joy, adventure, and much else that help us grow in faith'.

In the 1950s, it was smaller and printed in black and white with a picture of the church on the front. As printing facilities developed, the magazine added coloured covers. Included also were the yellow pages which give the dates and times of the various church services, activities and meetings; one page is reserved especially for the Rector's notices and he is delightfully cartooned. Other information includes articles written by church members together with local business adverts which help to pay for printing.

# The Register

*The Register* started as a sister magazine to the *Wyke Register* which had been published by Artsmiths on Portland since May 1991. Iain Ross, who grew up in Wyke Regis but now lives in Preston, took over the *Wyke Register* in February 2005, and as he had always thought there was scope for a magazine covering the Preston area, launched *The Register* in November 2005, covering Preston, Sutton Poyntz, Osmington and Osmington Mills. Both magazines were originally printed in black and white, but in November 2006 both were printed with a full colour section on gloss paper for the first time. Delivered door-to-door each month by a commercial distributer and also available in local shops, the *Registers* are widely read and well received for their articles, advertisements and the opportunity for local people to write about and share their interests, events and experiences. Recently the *Wyke Register* reached issue 259 and *The Register* issue 85, and long may they continue. With the Jurassic coast and wonderful countryside on the doorstep, Iain's love of landscape photography is showcased each month on the front covers of both magazines.

# Night School

On 16 October 1900 an Evening Continuation School was opened in the old school by the church to serve pupils from Sutton Poyntz and Preston, the timetable approved by H.M. Inspector of Schools. It had four managers – the Misses Williams from Osmington House in Weymouth, Capt. Mould and the Rev. E. Henslowe – together with a teacher Mr Henry E. Burch who held a trainee certificate. Twelve members were admitted, their ages ranging from 13 to 30 years. Subjects taught were Commercial Arithmetic, Geography and later Science, the managers having provided copies of *Blackie's Complete Arithmetic* and *Geography of the British Isles*. Lantern lectures on places such as Canada were also included.

All was going well until January 1902 when the disorderly conduct of some of the scholars ended with closure of the school. Fortunately, the pupils voluntarily apologised; they had learnt their lesson. The following was recorded in the school Log Book: 'discipline is a matter of individual effort rather than the result of rules ... and therefore the shutting of the school, although to be deplored, has taught them a valuable lesson'.

In August 1905 one of the Miss Williams sisters kindly organised an outing to Bristol for the boys, sixteen of whom had achieved a regular attendance. In 1906, Plane and Solid Geometry was added to the list of subjects as an introduction to Building Construction.

## *St Andrew's School*

Closely linked to St Andrew's Church, the village school and school house (where the headmaster lived) were built around 1850, tucked away behind the Spice Ship. What is now a very old Log Book, its pages yellow with age and edges frayed, kept track of daily events. The book was filled with spidery copperplate hand-writing in pen and black ink, and daily records were kept on behaviour, progress and attendance. Children were frequently sent home with sickness, fever or head-lice. Some were unable to attend since they were needed at home if the mother was sick and they were required to look after younger siblings, or to carry food to their fathers potato-picking in the fields. Sometimes absence was due to very wet weather or when the children's shoes were at the cobblers. Telling falsehoods, being late for school, laughing during prayers and copying another's work were all punishable, sometimes by writing lines of poetry or learning twelve or more lines to be recited later to the teacher.

The surnames of some of the pupils at this time included Burt, White, Butler, Galphin, Read, Pickett, Notley, Hellier, Plowman, Keynes, Hallett, Elliot, Scriven, Whittle, King and Goldring. There were four classes: infants, 7–9 year olds, 8–11 year olds and the senior children up to age 14. Those who failed their scholarship were sent to Broadwey Secondary School, now Wey Valley. Later, at the age of 13, it became possible to sit a test for admission to the Technical School in Weymouth.

Grace and prayers were read each morning followed by RE, or Scripture lesson as it was called then. Being a church school the Creed and the Twelve Commandments were learnt by heart and the Rector visited once a week. There were playgrounds for each individual group, and classrooms were small with a blackboard and easel at the front together with a coke-fired stove. A doctor came regularly to check sight and hearing, and a nurse checked for the ubiquitous head-louse. Multiplication tables were learned by heart, from 2 to 12 in those days when 12 inches made 1 ft and 12 pence made a shilling. Male teachers were not averse to throwing chalk at inattentive pupils or caning boys for bad work or behaviour.

With increasing numbers of children, a new school on Littlemoor Road was opened in November 1991 by the Rev. John Kirkham, Bishop of Sherborne. The old school buildings stood empty for some years before they were eventually purchased and turned into a spacious and beautiful home, well tucked away.

The present St Andrew's Primary School holds around 370 children aged 5–11 and a teaching staff of 16 covering 14 classes. The school is seen as a hub of the community, working closely with other professions. In spite of the Head Teacher's heavy managerial and professional responsibilities, she makes time to teach as well, through which she comes to know personally and individually the children in her care. With so many parents working now, the school also offers breakfast and after-school clubs, as well as extra-curricular activities.

## *Exploring on foot*

A delightful place for walking, Preston boasts flat areas and coastal stretches, together with hills and clifftops – on fine days it is possible to see both far inland and out to sea, even to the Isle of Wight. The popular and well-walked South West Coastal Path splits just south-east of Osmington, the inland stretch running along the South Dorset Ridgeway to rejoin the coastal section a few miles on at Osmington Mills. The coastal path in Preston suffers periodically especially after a hard, wet winter when landslip causes breaks in the track and rerouting is required.

Walks ranging from a few miles to ten or more can be made easily in the Preston area for there is a network of paths that cover the coastline, ridge, Chalbury Hill and countryside in between.

### And finally …

*With so much history behind it, and inspiring scenery all around,*
*with supportive but not intruding neighbours,*
*with cheerful bus drivers who not only share a joke*
*but wait for those running for the bus*
*and pause until their passengers are seated,*
*where local children are charming and well-behaved,*
*and adults who not only smile at you but pass the time of day,*
*Preston is a happy place in which to live and to retire*
*and long may this continue.*

# Other Roving Press Titles

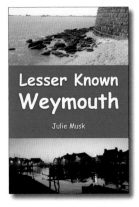

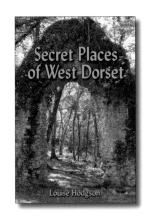

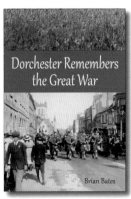

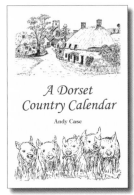

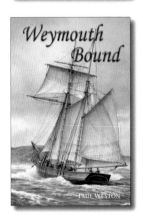

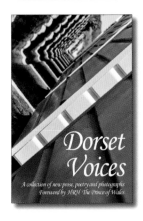

Roving Press

*If you like exploring, you'll love our books*